CAN ELEPHANTS DRINK THROUGH THEIR NOSES?

CAN ELEPHANTS DRINK THROUGH THEIR NOSES?

The strange things people say
about animals at the zoo

by Deborah Dennard
illustrated by Terry Boles

Carolrhoda Books, Inc. / Minneapolis

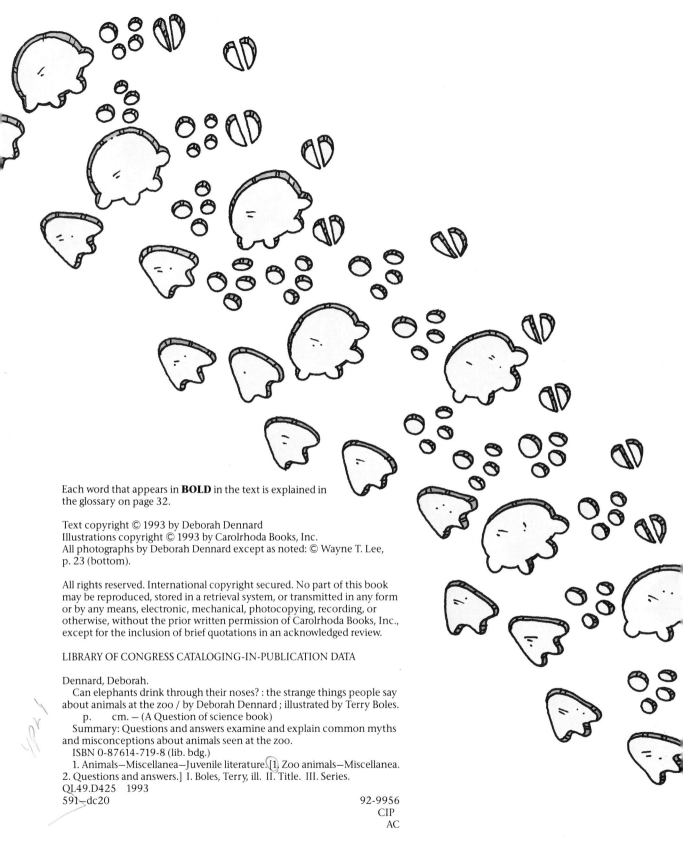

Each word that appears in **BOLD** in the text is explained in
the glossary on page 32.

Text copyright © 1993 by Deborah Dennard
Illustrations copyright © 1993 by Carolrhoda Books, Inc.
All photographs by Deborah Dennard except as noted: © Wayne T. Lee,
p. 23 (bottom).

LIBRARY OF CONGRESS CATALOGING-IN-PUBLICATION DATA

Dennard, Deborah.
    Can elephants drink through their noses? : the strange things people say
about animals at the zoo / by Deborah Dennard ; illustrated by Terry Boles.
        p.   cm. — (A Question of science book)
    Summary: Questions and answers examine and explain common myths
and misconceptions about animals seen at the zoo.
    ISBN 0-87614-719-8 (lib. bdg.)
    1. Animals—Miscellanea—Juvenile literature. [1. Zoo animals—Miscellanea.
2. Questions and answers.] I. Boles, Terry, ill. II. Title. III. Series.
QL49.D425   1993
591—dc20   92-9956
                                                                    CIP
                                                                    AC

Manufactured in the United States of America

1 2 3 4 5 6 98 97 96 95 94 93

For Deb and Barry—*D.D.*

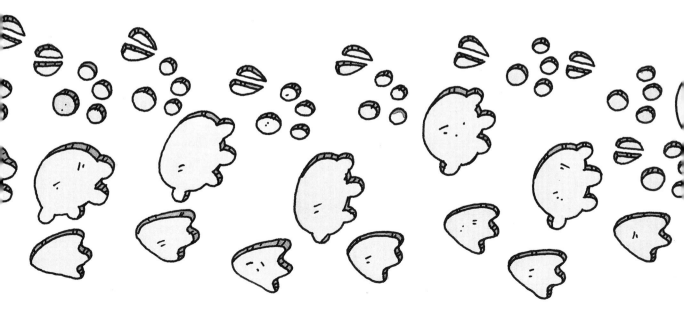

So, how do elephants drink?

Are gorillas fierce monsters?

And does a camel hold water in its hump?

If you think you already know all the answers, think again. The truth about animals at the zoo isn't always what you might expect. People have some pretty funny ideas about zoo animals. Not all of these ideas are true.

Let's take a look at some things people say about animals. Will you agree?

Many people say that elephants drink through their noses. Do you think so too?

The answer is yes and no. An elephant's trunk is part nose and part upper lip. It stretches out like a long, moving tube. When an elephant drinks, it sucks as much as three gallons of water into its trunk. But an elephant can't swallow the water from there. To swallow, it has to squirt the water out of its trunk and into its mouth. Elephants also squirt water onto their backs to take a shower!

Is it true that elephants never forget?

Elephants are powerful and smart. They can be taught to do hard work, pulling, pushing, and carrying. They are sometimes trained to do circus tricks. Elephants learn quickly and seem to like their jobs. Maybe that's why people say elephants never forget. But since people and elephants can't talk to each other, no one really knows.

Do people forget? Sometimes.
Do elephants forget? Probably.

Are all zebra stripes the same?

Zebra stripes are as different as human fingerprints. No two zebras have exactly the same color and pattern of stripes. In a **herd** of zebras, it's hard to tell where one animal ends and the next begins. Stripes confuse **predators,** such as lions and cheetahs, that kill and feed on zebras. Stripes help zebras stay alive.

Are gorillas angry giants?

Gorillas may weigh 400 pounds, but they are gentle animals. Gorillas in the wild live far from people, deep in the forests of Africa. When frightened, they pound their chests in warning. They may even throw sticks in the air to scare away other animals. But real gorillas are not like monster gorillas you see in movies and cartoons. Real gorillas hardly ever fight. In fact, their best defense is to hide.

If gorillas aren't big monsters, are they just big monkeys?

MOM   DAD   JR.

Gorillas and monkeys are different, and the difference
is easy to see. Monkeys have tails. Gorillas, chimpan-
zees, and other apes do not have tails. Just the same,
gorillas, apes, and monkeys are related. They are all
part of a group of animals called **primates.**

Many people say camels store water in their humps. Do you agree?

In the wild, camels live in hot, dry deserts far from water. When camels do find water, they drink a lot! Water stays in fat under the camel's skin. Water is stored all over the camel's body, not just in its hump. Once a camel has had a good, long drink, it can go for many days without drinking again.

Why doesn't a camel sink into the sand when it walks in the desert?

A camel's feet are very big, round, and flat on the bottom. They act like snowshoes made for sand. Camels' feet spread their weight out so that camels can walk easily on sand.

Do llamas spit on people they don't like?

Llamas spit, but usually at other llamas, not at people. Llamas spit when they are scared. Spitting is a way llamas defend themselves. When near people who are quiet and gentle, llamas have no reason to spit.

Some people say that giraffes are always silent.
Do you think so too?

The tallest animal in the world is quiet most of the time, but not all of the time. Soft, low moans are the most common noises made by giraffes. Baby giraffes make a funny bleating sound, like a lamb with a sore throat.

Are lions king of the jungle?

Lions in zoos don't live in jungles, and neither do lions in the wild. In fact, lions in the wild live on grasslands, open grassy places with few trees.

Lions seem to sleep all day long. Are they lazy?

Lions sleep 18 to 20 hours every day! But lions are not lazy. When lions in the wild hunt, they eat until they are very, very full. Then they sleep and rest for several days until they are hungry again.

Lions can't be king of a place where they don't live. If lions are king of anywhere, they are king of the grasslands. And since female lions are the best hunters, it might be better to say that lions are *queen* of the grasslands.

Do ostriches hide their heads in the sand?

Why do people think ostriches hide their heads in the sand? Like many other animals, ostriches take dust baths. They lie flat on the ground with their necks stretched out in front. Then they clean themselves by throwing dust on their backs. Bits of dust act like tiny scrubbers. The dust rubs feathers and skin clean. Ostriches don't *hide* their heads in the sand. They *clean* their heads in the sand!

Some birds at the zoo don't live in cages. Why don't they just fly away?

Flamingos can fly hundreds and hundreds of miles. But most flamingos in zoos don't fly. Why not? The wings of many zoo birds, such as flamingos, are clipped short on one side. This puts the birds off balance. Zoo flamingos can't fly, even though wild flamingos can.

Some people say koalas are the cuddliest bears of all. Do you think so too?

Koalas may look cute and cuddly, but they aren't bears at all. Koalas are from Australia. Like kangaroos, they have pouches of skin for holding their young. Both koalas and kangaroos are part of a group of animals with pouches called **marsupials.**

How about pandas?
Are they bears too?

Pandas from China look bear-like, but they aren't bears. They aren't marsupials either, since they don't have pouches. In fact, no one knows for sure what pandas are. They may be giant raccoons!

So, can penguins fly?

Are killer whales really killers?

And do crocodiles cry crocodile tears?

If you think you know all about animals at the zoo, just remember, animals are not always as they seem. To find out the truth about animals, keep asking questions! The answers are sure to surprise you.

GLOSSARY

herd: A group of a certain kind of animal living, feeding, and traveling together. Zebras live in a herd. So do elephants. Herds are nature's proof that there is safety in numbers.

marsupial: Animals with pouches of skin. Inside their pouches, marsupials give their babies food, warmth, milk, and safety. Koalas, kangaroos, and opossums are marsupials. Baby marsupials are very tiny and helpless when first born. They spend up to a year growing in their mothers' pouch.

predator: Animals that hunt and kill other animals for food. Lions, tigers, and bears are predators. So are spiders, snakes, and sharks.

primate: The group of warm-blooded animals including monkeys, apes, and people. There are about 200 kinds of primates. They range in size from a kind of monkey that weighs less than 1 pound to gorillas that weigh as much as 400 pounds.